My Big Wipe Clean Reading

3+

Reading

duck hat cat

Over 40 fun activities!

This book belongs to:

_____

(Don't worry if you can't write your name now – you'll
be able to once you've finished this book!)

The Alphabet

There are 26 letters in the alphabet. They all make different sounds. Can you follow the lines to write all the letters below? Then try to remember the sound each letter makes.

Start each letter at the big dot.

Vowel Snake

Write the missing letters of the alphabet in the spaces below.
Do you know what the missing letters are called?

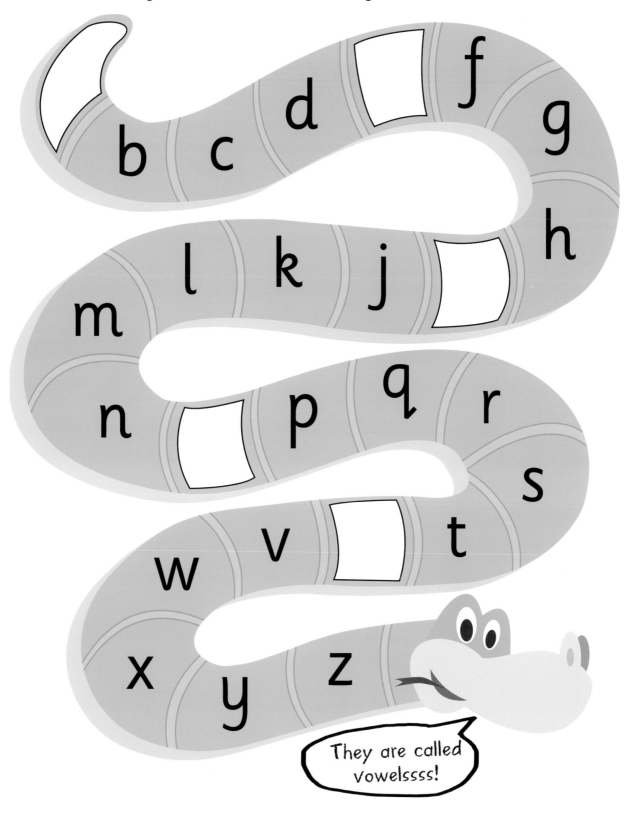

They are called vowelssss!

The 'A' Family

Here's how to write lower-case 'a':

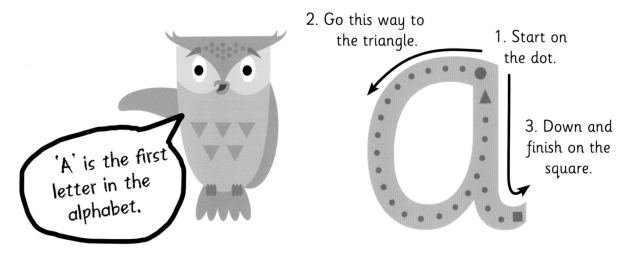

2. Go this way to the triangle.

1. Start on the dot.

3. Down and finish on the square.

'A' is the first letter in the alphabet.

Now try tracing these:

a a a a a a a

All of these words have an 'a' sound in the middle. Write 'a' in the gaps to complete the words, then read them all out loud.

r_t   f_n

m_n   n_p

c_p   h_t

Cat on the Mat

Read the sentence below, then read the sentences underneath and circle the correct words to complete them.

The fat cat sat on the blue mat, in a black hat.

The cat sat on the step / mat.

The cat is thin / fat.

The mat is blue / green.

The cat is wearing a tie / hat.

The hat is brown / black.

The 'E' Family

Here's how to write lower-case 'e':

You write 'e' by drawing a little spiral.

2. Go up...

3. ... and around to the square.

1. Start on this dot.

Now try tracing these:

All of these words have an 'e' sound in the middle. Write 'e' in the gaps to complete the words, then read them all out loud.

p _ n   w _ t

g _ t   l _ g

b _ d   h _ n

Word Pyramids

The words in these pyramids are all missing their 'e's. Trace the letters and fill in the missing 'e's, then read all the words out loud.

The 'I' Family

Heres how to write lower-case 'i':

The little 'i' is special because it has a little dot.

1. Start on this dot.

2. Go around to the square.

3. Finish with a little dot here!

Now try tracing these:

All of these words have an 'i' sound in the middle. Write 'i' in the gaps to complete the words, then read them all out loud.

w _ n   l _ p

b _ n   b _ g

p _ g   s _ t

Circle the Words

Look at the pictures below, then read the sentences next to them.
Use your pen to circle the correct word in each sentence.

The fish is
pink / orange.

The pig is
pink / orange.

The ant is
big / little.

The elephant
is big / little.

The 'O' Family

Here's how to write lower-case 'o':

The letter 'o' is a circle.

1. Start here...

2. ... and go around until you're back where you began.

Now try tracing these:

O O O O O O O

All of these words have an 'o' sound in the middle.
Write 'o' in the gaps to complete the words, then read the words out loud.

d _ g   t _ p

l _ g   h _ t

fr _ g   l _ t

Complete the Cross

Using the nine letters below, see how many different three-letter 'o' words you can make. We've helped you with the first one. Can you complete all five crosses?

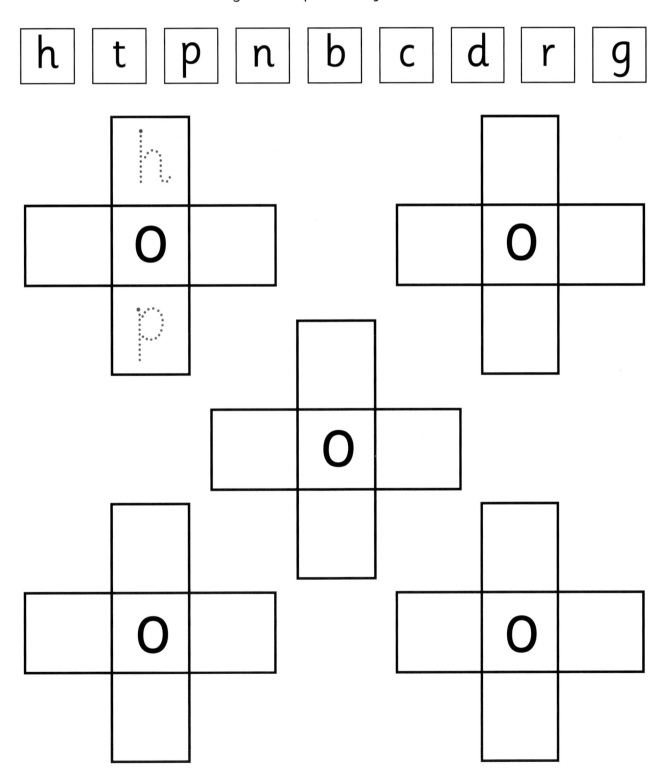

The 'U' Family

Lower-case 'u' is one of the letters with a tail:

'U' did it!

1. Start on this dot.

2. Go around to here...

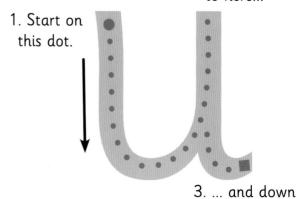

3. ... and down to finish!

Now try tracing these:

u   u   u   u   u   u   u

All of these words have a 'u' sound in the middle.
Write 'u' in the gaps to complete the words, then read the words out loud.

dr _ m   r _ b

j _ g   j _ mp

s _ n   b _ n

What Can U Find?

Let's see how many more 'u' words you know. Using your pen, circle all the 'u' words in the giant letter 'u' below.

I found ☐ different 'u' words.

Odd One Out

In each line of words below, there is one word that doesn't have the same middle sound. Read the words out loud, then use your pen to circle the odd one out.

fan / dog / bag / bad

cup / hut / pin / run

dot / job / top / rat

lip / leg / peg / get

bus / mug / bin / bun

pig / pip / pop / pit

man / hat / dad / got

Keep it up!

You're doing a great job!

Read a Rainbow

Do you know the colours of the rainbow? Fill in the missing vowels to complete the colours below, then answer Molly's question!

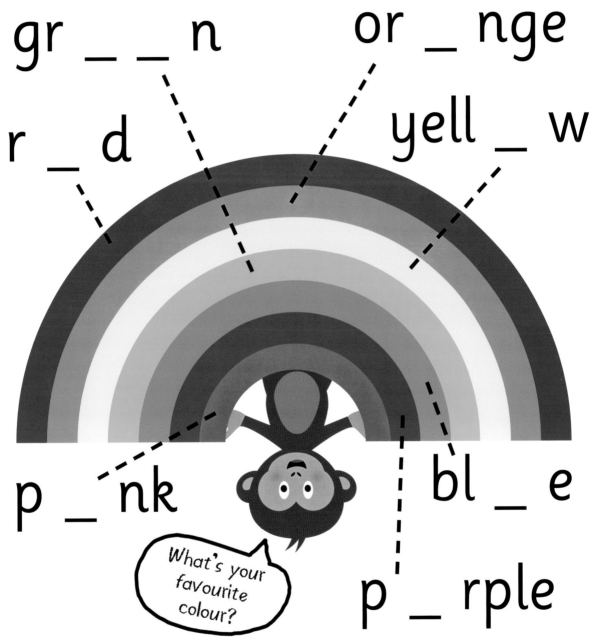

gr _ _ n

or _ nge

r _ d

yell _ w

p _ nk

bl _ e

What's your favourite colour?

p _ rple

My favourite colour is:

....

Animal Sounds

These noisy animals are all talking using double vowels.
Can you trace the letters below, then read the noises they make?

Vowel Maze

Can you remember which five letters are called vowels? This fussy beaver only likes to walk on vowels. Can you draw a path using only vowels to take him to the handy log?

Start

a	e	m	l	f	h
g	i	o	b	t	x

m	c	b	k	u	m	v	j
d	f	i	e	a	c	y	w
g	u	o	n	d	h	l	z
j	a	h	u	a	e	r	m
b	e	i	o	p	i		
c	k	m	q	s	o		

Finish

Molly and Woody

A cheeky monkey has taken the vowels from this story! Can you put the vowels back in the right places, then read the story out loud?

M _ lly the monk _ y lives in a tr _ e. Her h _ me is a n _ st of tw _ gs and leaves. One d _ y, she found an owl c _ lled W _ ody in h _ r n _ st.

"Don't w _ rry," she t _ ld h _ m. "You c _ n share my n _ st!"

All About Woody

Read the text about Woody, then use your pen to circle the correct words in the sentences underneath.

Woody is an owl.
His favourite colour is red, and his best friend is called Molly.
Molly is a monkey.

Woody is an owl / ant.

Molly is a mouse / monkey.

Woody's favourite colour is red / blue.

Woody's best friend is called Molly / Holly.

Tim the Tiger

Read the story about Tim the tiger, then use your pen
to write in the answers to the questions below.

Tim the tiger was very sad.
He had lost his favourite hat!
"I know where it is," said Pippa the
parrot. "Your hat is on your head!"
Tim put his paws
on his head and
found his hat.
Now he felt happy.

What is the tiger's name? ....

What has the tiger lost? ....

How did the tiger feel
at the start of the story? ....

How did the tiger feel
at the end of the story? ....

Consonant Caterpillar

The letters that are not vowels are called consonants. Can you trace the dotted consonants below, then write the missing consonants in the gaps?

Picnic Mix-up

Molly and Woody are going on a picnic. Can you help them pack? Fill in the missing consonants in the words below, then draw lines to match them to the correct pictures.

cheese

ice cream

orange

milk

apple

'B', 'C', 'D' and 'F'

The first four consonants in the alphabet are 'b', 'c', 'd' and 'f'.
You can make lots of useful words by using them with the right vowels.
First, let's practise writing them.

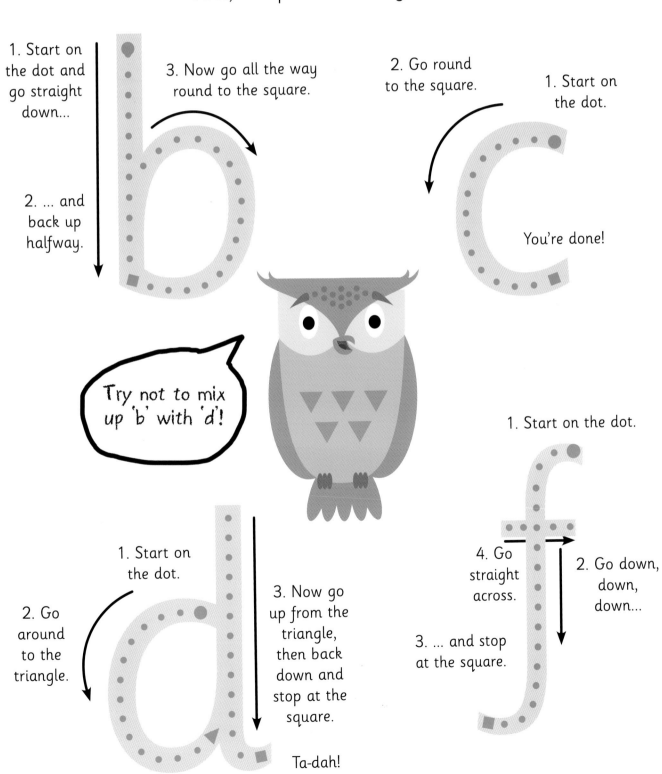

1. Start on the dot and go straight down...

2. ... and back up halfway.

3. Now go all the way round to the square.

2. Go round to the square.

1. Start on the dot.

You're done!

Try not to mix up 'b' with 'd'!

1. Start on the dot.

2. Go around to the triangle.

3. Now go up from the triangle, then back down and stop at the square.

Ta-dah!

1. Start on the dot.

2. Go down, down, down...

3. ... and stop at the square.

4. Go straight across.

This is a...

Read the sentences below and use your pen to fill in the missing letters. Then circle the right word on each line to make the sentences match the pictures.

This is a bird / bee.

This is a cat / cow.

This is a dog / duck.

This is a frog / fish.

'G', 'H', 'J' and 'K'

The next four consonants are 'g', 'h', 'j' and 'k'. Can you remember the sounds they make? Say them out loud, then practise writing them.

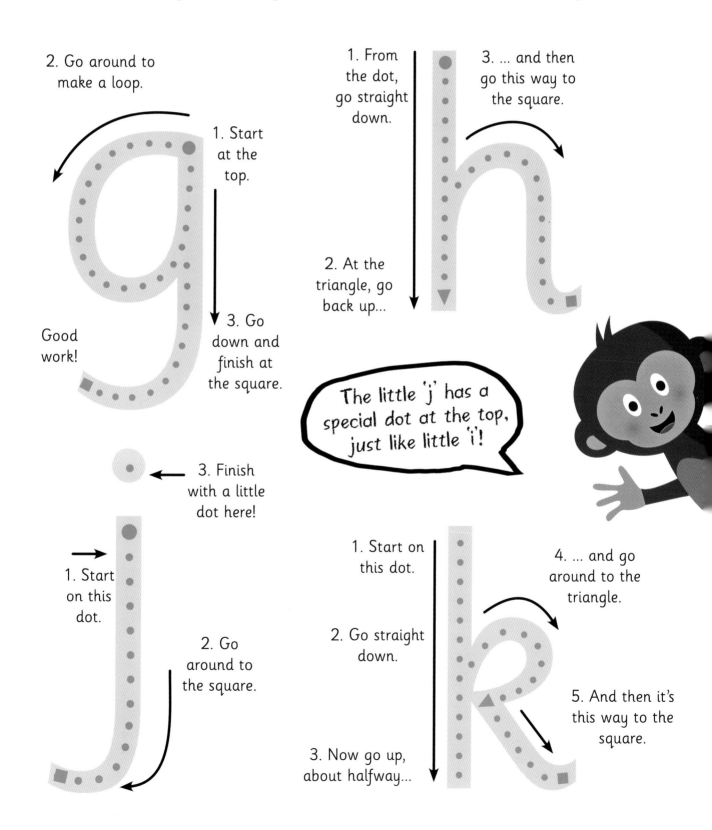

2. Go around to make a loop.

1. Start at the top.

Good work!

3. Go down and finish at the square.

1. From the dot, go straight down.

3. ... and then go this way to the square.

2. At the triangle, go back up...

The little 'j' has a special dot at the top, just like little 'i'!

3. Finish with a little dot here!

1. Start on this dot.

2. Go around to the square.

1. Start on this dot.

2. Go straight down.

3. Now go up, about halfway...

4. ... and go around to the triangle.

5. And then it's this way to the square.

Missing Letters

Each of the sentences below is missing either a 'g', 'h', 'j' or 'k'. Can you work out which letters are missing, then write them in with your pen to complete the sentences?

The _rass is _reen.

The _en is _appy.

The _ellyfish is _olly.

The _ing is _ind.

'L', 'M', 'N' and 'P'

Are you ready for four more consonants? Try reading 'l', 'm', 'n' and 'p', then follow the instructions below to write the letters.

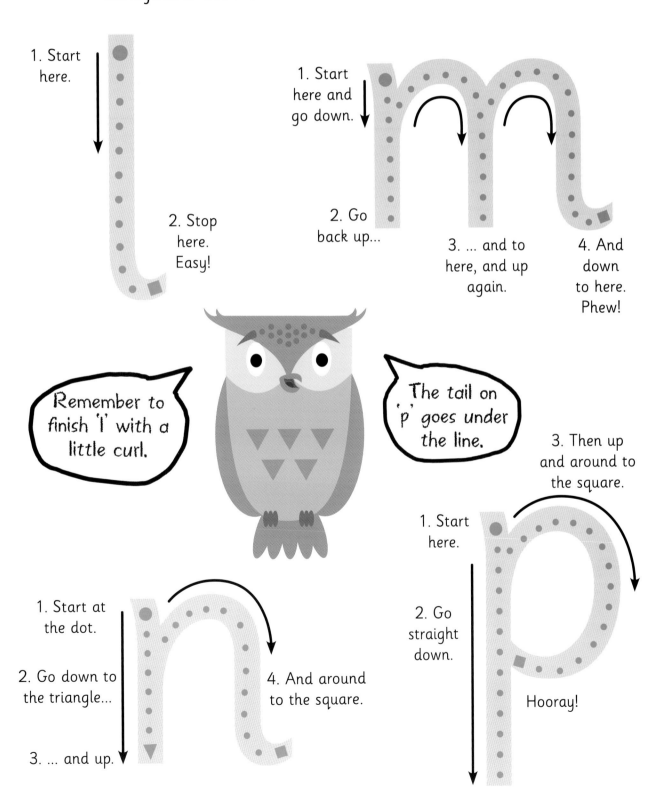

1. Start here.

2. Stop here. Easy!

1. Start here and go down.

2. Go back up...

3. ... and to here, and up again.

4. And down to here. Phew!

Remember to finish 'l' with a little curl.

The tail on 'p' goes under the line.

3. Then up and around to the square.

1. Start here.

2. Go straight down.

Hooray!

1. Start at the dot.

2. Go down to the triangle...

3. ... and up.

4. And around to the square.

Fruit Salad

Woody wants to make a fruit salad, but some of the letters have faded away! Use your pen to fill in the missing 'l', 'm', 'n' or 'p' to complete these fruity words, then read them out loud.

banana   lemon

plum   melon

nectarine   pear

peach   pineapple

mango   lime

How many of each letter did you write?

l ☐   fm ☐   n ☐   p ☐

'Q', 'R', 'S' and 'T'

Now it's time to meet 'q', 'r', 's' and 't'. Use your pen to practise writing them all neatly.

Word Building

Sometimes, you can put two words together to make a new word. These are called compound words. Use your pen to match up the words below to create some compound words.

week	flower
quick	bow
rain	brush
sun	sand
tooth	end

'V', 'W', 'X', 'Y', 'Z'

The last five letters of the alphabet are all consonants. Follow Molly's advice below to learn how to write them all neatly.

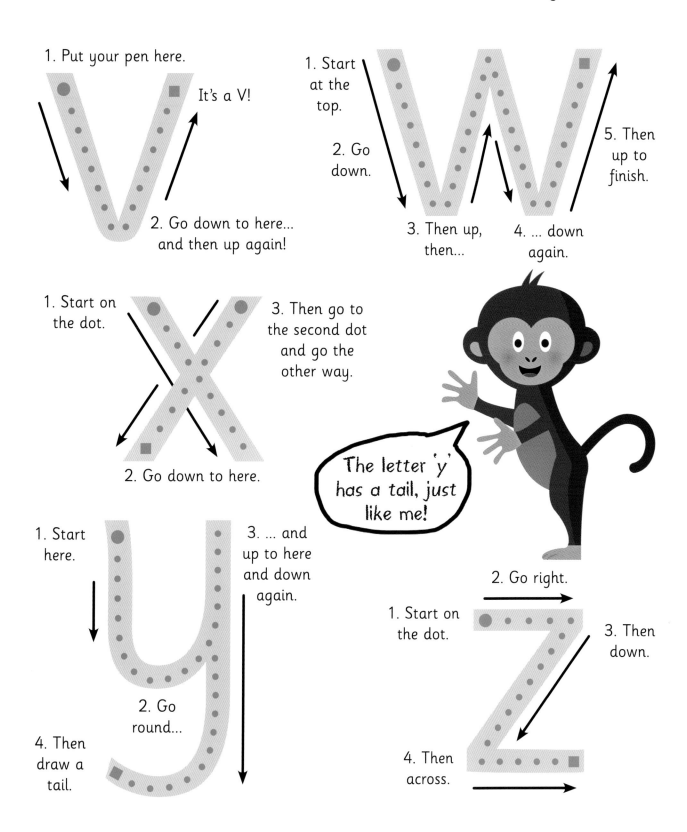

1. Put your pen here.

It's a V!

2. Go down to here... and then up again!

1. Start at the top.

2. Go down.

3. Then up, then...

4. ... down again.

5. Then up to finish.

1. Start on the dot.

3. Then go to the second dot and go the other way.

2. Go down to here.

The letter 'y' has a tail, just like me!

1. Start here.

3. ... and up to here and down again.

2. Go round...

4. Then draw a tail.

2. Go right.

1. Start on the dot.

3. Then down.

4. Then across.

What's in a Name?

Now that you've learnt all about vowels and consonants, write your name below and count how many of each you have in your name.

I've got 2 vowels and 3 consonants in my name! How many do you have?

Name:

Woody

Name:
....

Number of vowels: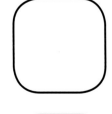

Number of consonants:

Vowel or Consonant?

Uh oh, all the vowels and consonants have been mixed up! Use your pen to sort the vowels and consonants into the correct boxes.

Vowels	Consonants

v k c l n p j q
d z i e t w h
o g u y s x b a f
m r

Where's the Vowel?

Vowels are very important. Almost every word needs at least one!
They can come at the beginning, middle or end of a word. Trace the
vowels below, then count up where they come in the words.

ant   ink   his

the   we   lip   spa

jog   hi   den   up

bus   owl   ask   fin

egg   hot   hop   pin

There are [ ] words with vowels at the beginning.

There are [ ] words with vowels in the middle.

There are [ ] words with vowels at the end.

Two-letter Grid

There are lots of two-letter words hidden in this grid. How many can you find? Use your pen to circle the words. You can go up, down, across or diagonally. The first one has been done for you.

d	a	w	h
o	i	n	e
f	t	s	u
b	e	o	p

Days of the Week

Molly has a busy week! Look at her calendar, then use your pen to write the correct day for each activity below.

Monday	drum lesson with Octopus
Tuesday	
Wednesday	cinema with Woody
Thursday	Unicorn's birthday party
Friday	day at the beach
Saturday	
Sunday	trip to the museum

Molly is visiting the museum on:

....

Molly has her drum lesson on:

....

Molly will be at the beach on:

....

Molly has no plans on:

....

Three-letter Words

There are lots of three-letter words hidden in this grid. How many can you find? Use your pen to circle the words. You can go up, down, across or diagonally. The first one has been done for you.

u	b	a	t	g
m	c	d	h	e
v	a	r	o	t
f	n	e	w	e
p	i	d	o	t

All About Molly

Read the text about Molly, then use your pen to circle the correct words in the sentences underneath.

Molly loves to sing. Her favourite food is bananas, and she plays the drums. She lives in a tree.

Molly loves to dance / sing.

Molly lives in a tree / hut.

Molly's favourite food is cheese / bananas.

Molly plays the drums / piano.

Treasure Hunt

Read the story, then use your pen to write three 'x's on the map,
to help Woody and Molly remember where they buried the treasure.

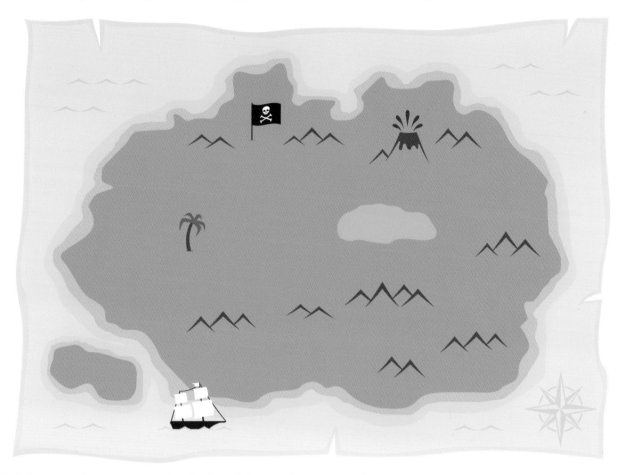

Woody and Molly found some treasure.
They went to an island to hide the
treasure. They hid the treasure in
three places. They buried some
treasure next to a tree,
behind a flag and
under a volcano.

Mark on the map
where we buried the
treasure so that we
can find it again!

Animal Jumble

Look at these pictures of Woody and Molly's animal friends.
Can you unscramble the letters to write the names of the animals?

pheleant

....

coniurn

....

topocus

....

kecnchi

....

Question Words

Question words are important words to learn, because they help you find things out! Trace the question words with your pen, then write the correct word next to each question.

who   when

what   where

why   how

_ _ _ _   time is it?

_ _ _ _   is your birthday?

_ _ _ _ _   are my keys?

_ _ _   are you feeling?

_ _ _   are you late?

_ _ _   is at the door?

Four-letter Words

There are lots of four-letter words hidden in this grid somewhere, how many can you find? Use your pen to circle the words. You can go up, down, across or diagonally. The first one has been done for you.

l	c	t	r	a	p
o	w	h	a	t	s
s	t	e	m	p	a
w	a	n	t	o	l
i	t	h	i	n	t
m	c	o	m	e	l

Word Search

Can you find all of the useful words below in the word search?
Remember, they might be written diagonally or even backwards!

they	some	people	little	their	house
what	then	that	said	have	called
asked	this	there	about	like	children
down	with	went	here	looked	

n	c	r	n	h	a	s	k	e	d
s	e	a	i	w	a	w	t	s	l
t	a	r	l	e	o	v	h	u	i
h	a	i	d	l	h	d	e	o	k
e	e	h	d	l	e	t	r	h	e
y	n	m	w	k	i	d	e	t	l
s	t	u	o	b	a	h	h	n	t
i	c	o	j	s	o	a	c	e	t
h	l	n	e	h	t	i	w	w	i
t	u	k	p	e	o	p	l	e	l

True or False

Read the sentences next to the pictures below. Use your pen to circle the tick or the cross, to show whether the sentences are true or false.

 The umbrella is yellow.

 This is a chicken.

 The hat is green.

 The boy is happy.

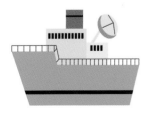 This is a giraffe.